3 DOORS DOWN

the better life

Transcribed by HEMME LUTTJEBOER

Project Managers: Jeannette DeLisa and Aaron Stang
Transcription Editor: Colgan Bryan
Book Art Layout: Thais Yanes
Album Artwork: © 1999 Universal Records Inc.
Photography: Andrew MacNaughtan
Album Art Direction/Design: PR Brown @ BAU - DA Design Lab, Inc.

IN DE GOOT
entertainment

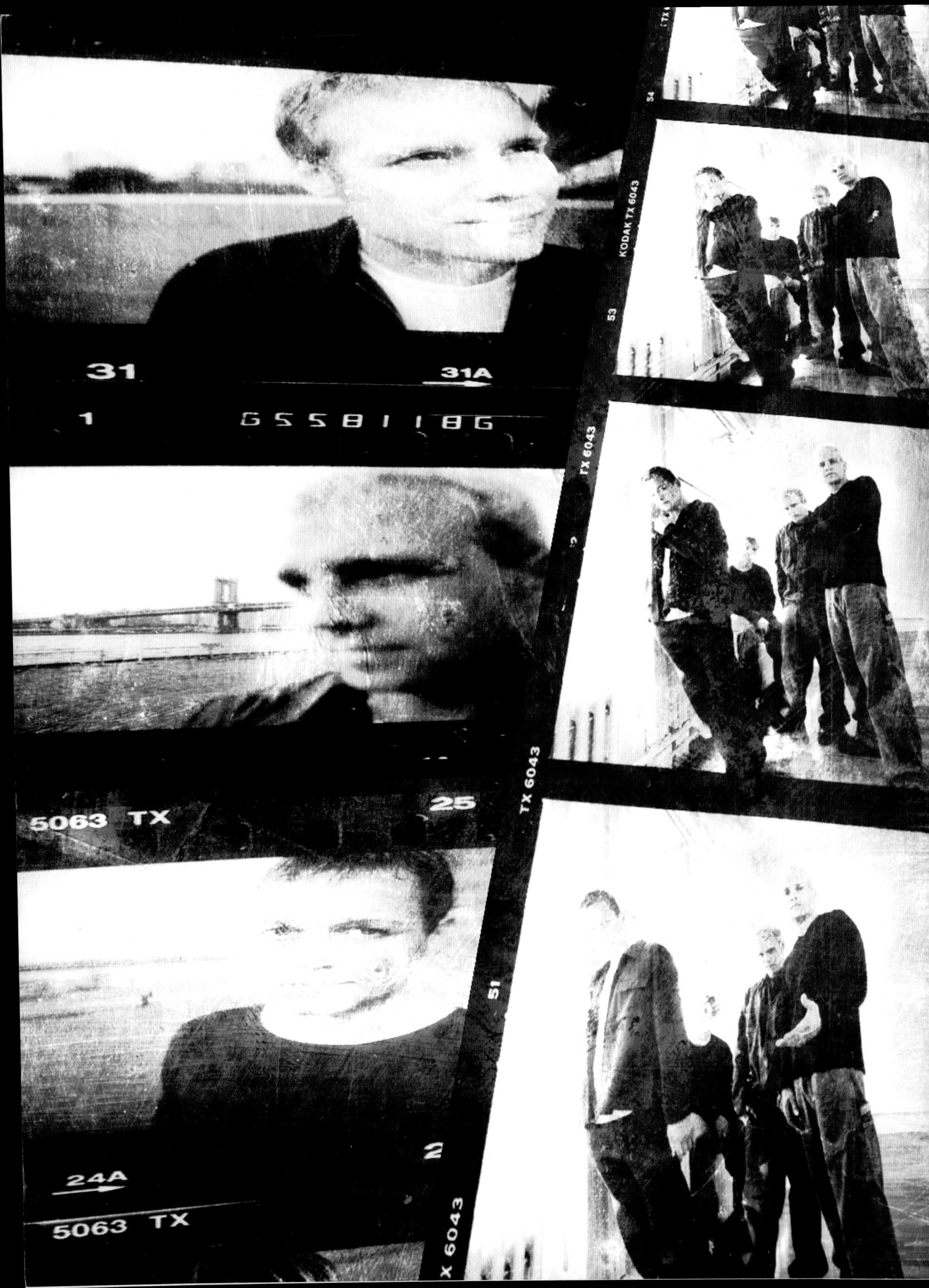

31
31A
1
5063 TX
25
24A
2
5063 TX
KODAK TX 6043
TX 6043
53
54
51

CONTENTS

KRYPTONITE

Music by MATT ROBERTS,
BRAD ARNOLD and TODD HARRELL
Lyrics by BRAD ARNOLD

6

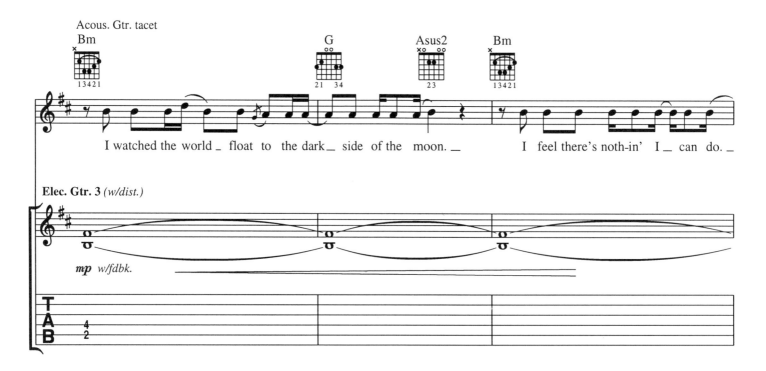

I watched the world _ float to the dark _ side of the moon. _   I feel there's noth-in' I _ can do. _

Interlude:

_ Yeah. _

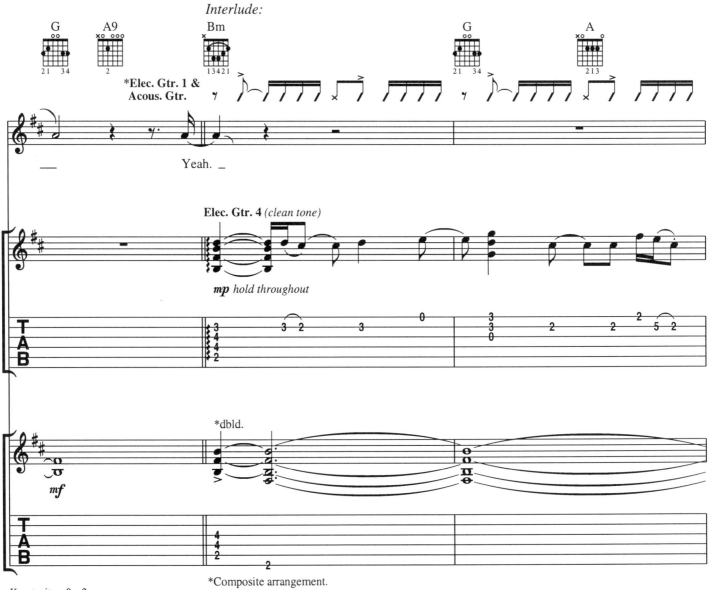

Composite arrangement.

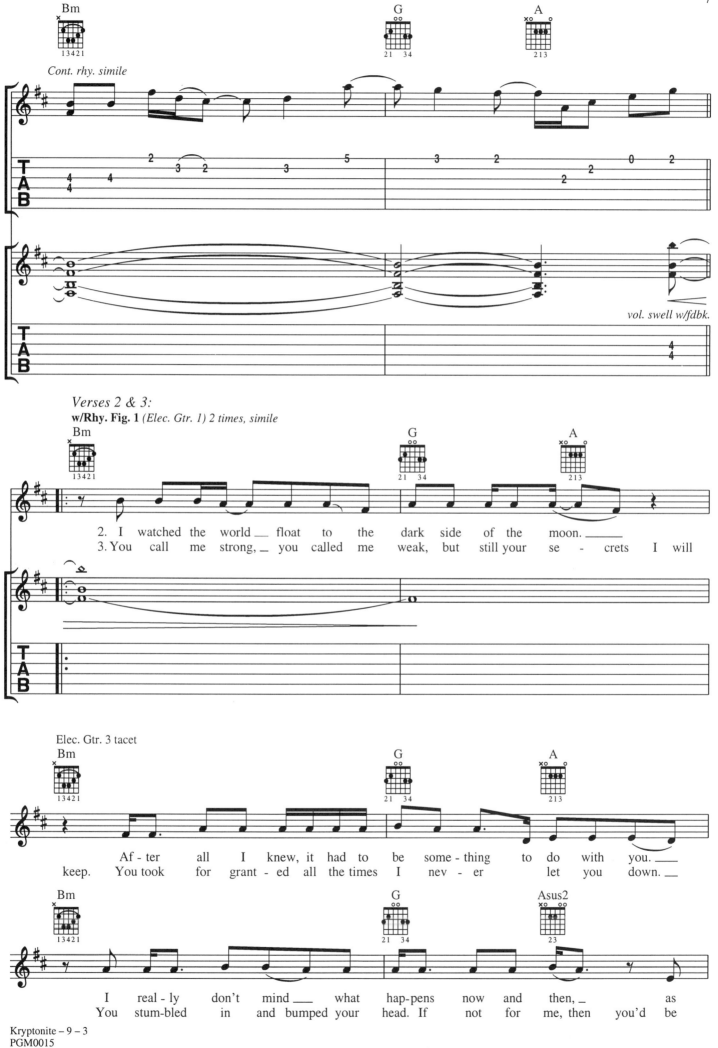

8

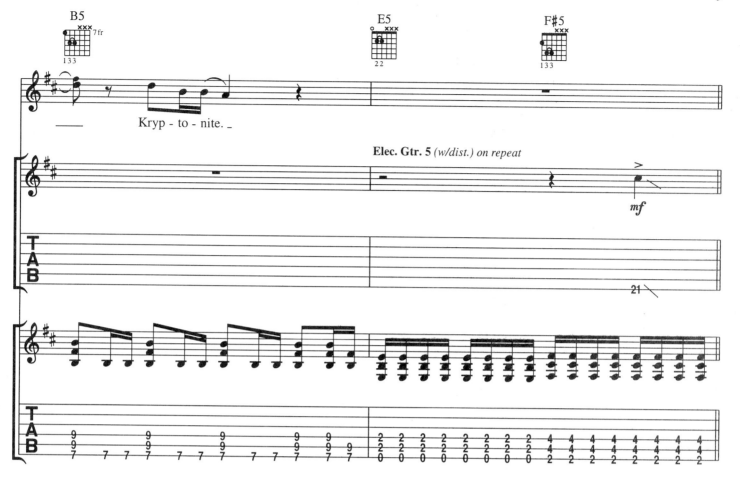

Kryp - to - nite. _

10

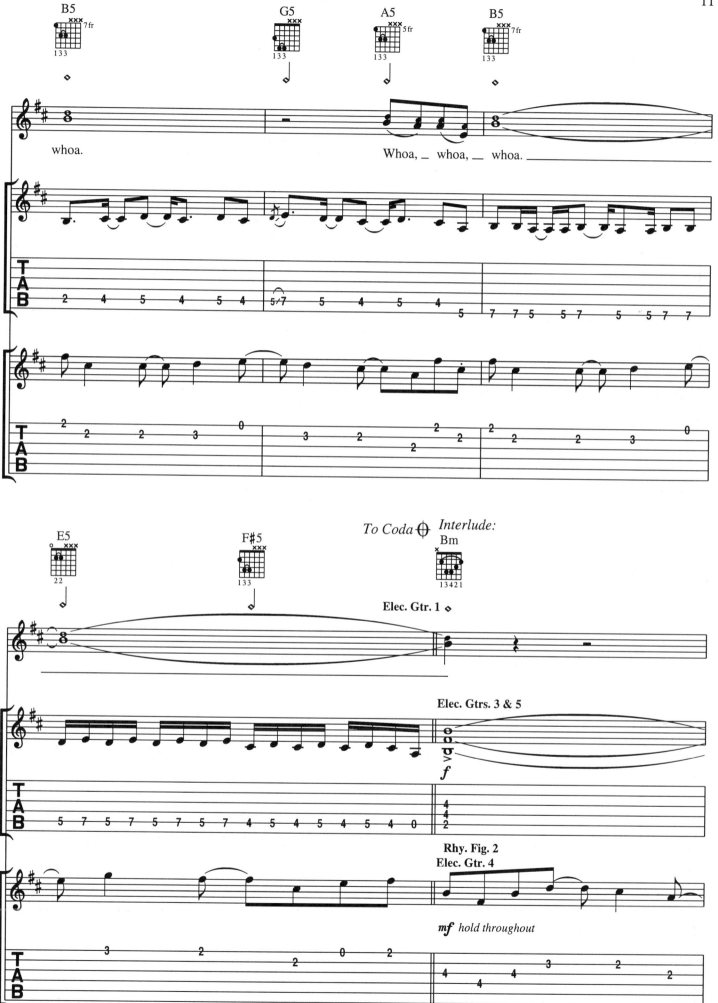

12

Chorus:

w/Rhy. Fig. 2 *(Elec. Gtr. 4) 2 times, simile*

If I go cra - zy, then will you still call me Su - per - man?_

If I'm a - live _ and well, will you be there hold-ing my hand?_ I'll keep you by my side with

Elec. Gtr. 1 & Acous. Gtr.

mp
hold throughout

Kryptonite – 9 – 8
PGM0015

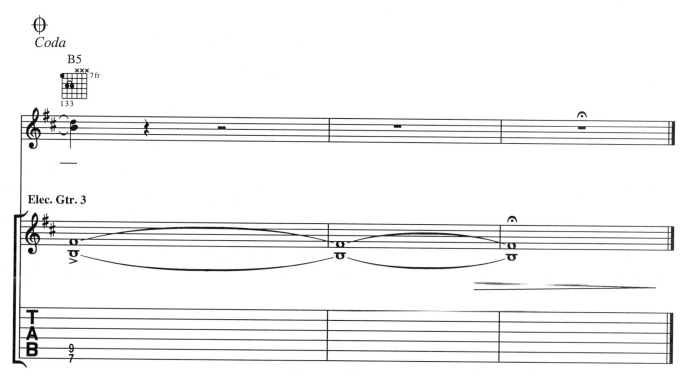

LOSER

Music by MATT ROBERTS,
BRAD ARNOLD and TODD HARRELL
Lyrics by BRAD ARNOLD

Slowly ♩ = 74

Intro:

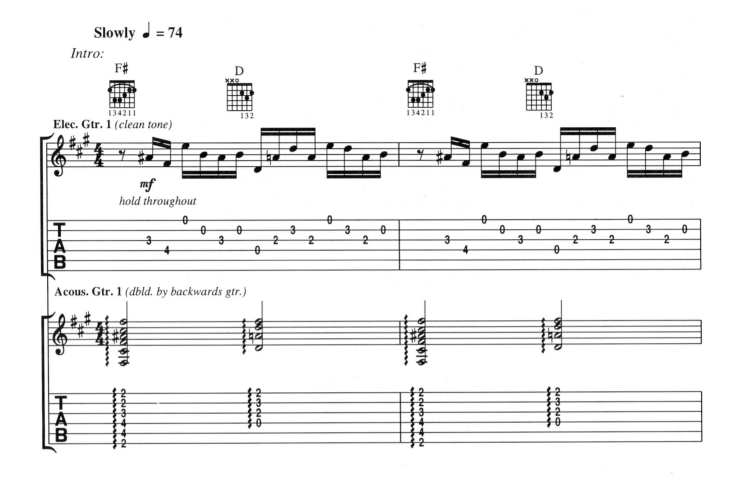

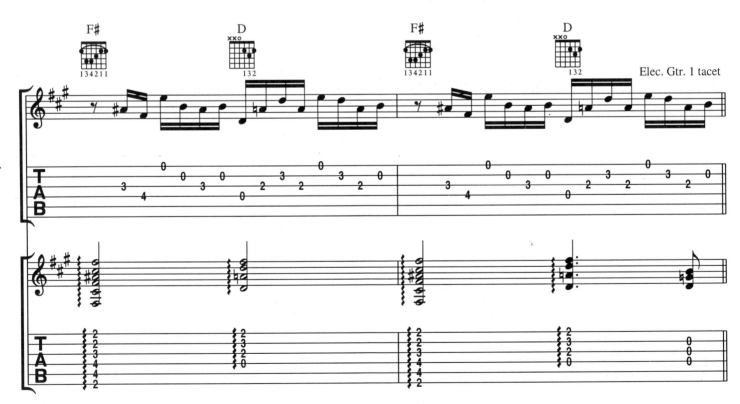

Loser – 8 – 1
PGM0015

16

*Composite arrangement.

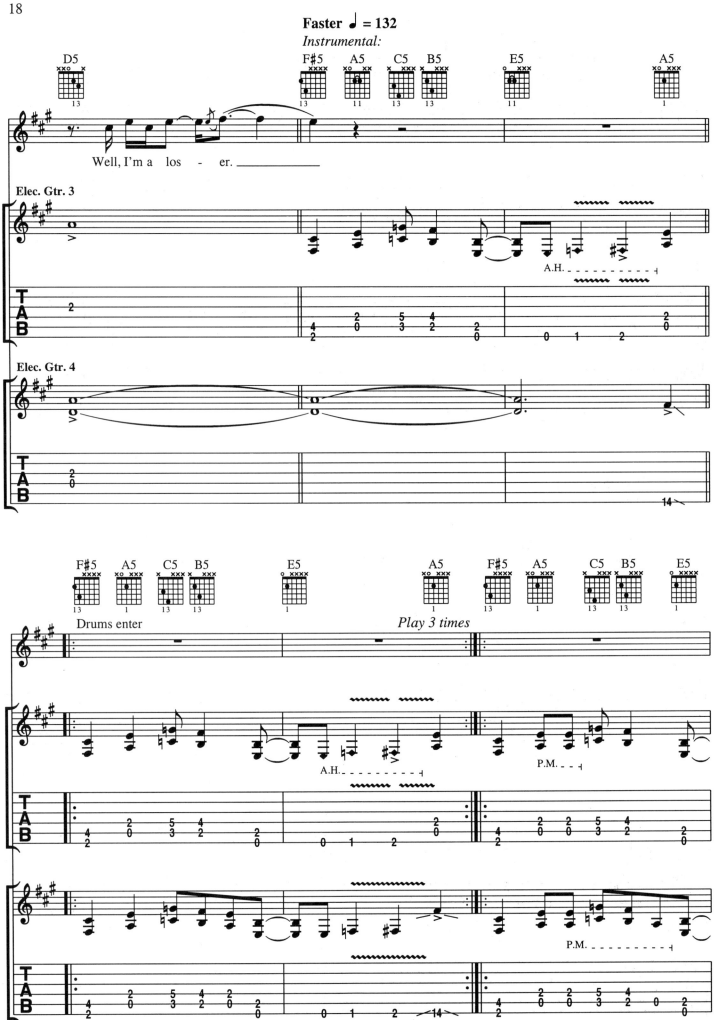

Well, I'm a los - er. _____

Outro Chorus:
w/Vcl. Fig. 1, *simile*
w/Rhy. Fig. 2 *(Elec. Gtrs. 3 & 4) simile*

(Lead vocal:) You're get-ting clos - er to push-in' me off __ of life's __ lit-tle edge. _____

Los - er, ba - by. __ The soon - er or lat - er, _____

yeah. __ You're hold-ing the rope __ and I'm tak - in', _____ I'm tak-

Elec. Gtr. 5 *(w/dist.)*

mp

- in', _____ I'm tak - in'. __ Yeah. _____

Elec. Gtrs. 3 & 4

DUCK AND RUN

Music by MATT ROBERTS, BRAD ARNOLD,
TODD HARRELL and CHRIS HENDERSON
Lyrics by BRAD ARNOLD

Acous. Gtr. 1 tune to Em tuning:

⑥ = E ③ = G
⑤ = B ② = B
④ = E ① = E

Moderate rock ♩ = 86

Intro:

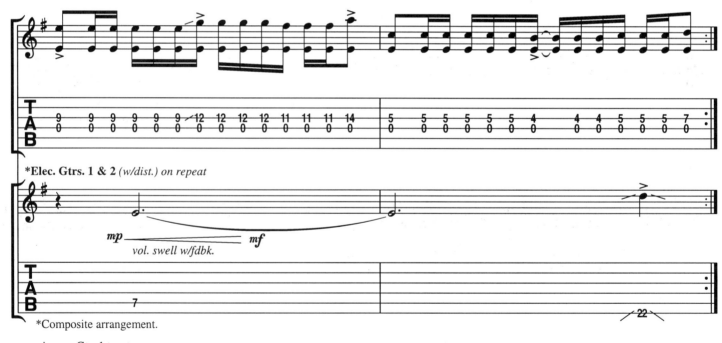

*Composite arrangement.

Acous. Gtr. 1 tacet

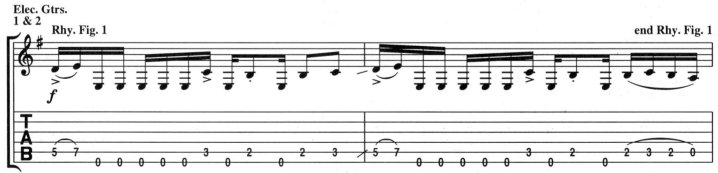

Duck and Run – 7 – 1
PGM0015

Verse:

w/Rhy. Fig. 1 *(Elec. Gtrs. 1 & 2) 4 times, simile*

E5

1. To this world I am un-im-por-tant ___ just be-cause I have ___ noth-ing ___ to give. ___
2. All my work and end-less mea-sures ___ nev-er seem to get me ver-y far. ___

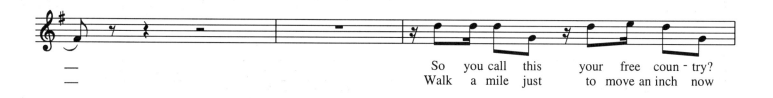

— So you call this your free coun-try?
— Walk a mile just to move an inch now

Tell me why it costs ___ so much ___ to live. ___   Tell ___ me why. _____
e-ven though I'm try-in' so damn hard. ___   I'm try-in' so hard. ___

Chorus:

Em   G   D/F#   C   Bm   C

Rhy. Fig. 2   **end Rhy. Fig. 2**

Elec.
Gtrs. 1 & 2
(dbld. by Acous. Gtr. 2)

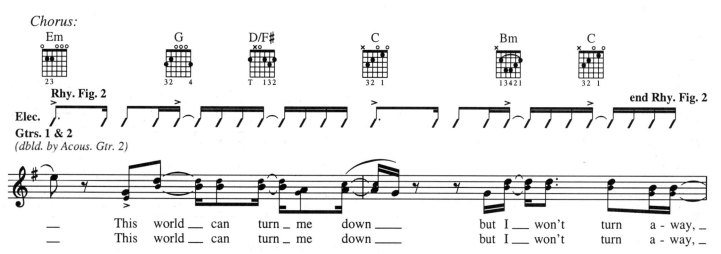

___ This world ___ can turn ___ me down ___ but I ___ won't turn a-way, ___
___ This world ___ can turn ___ me down ___ but I ___ won't turn a-way, ___

Duck and Run – 7 – 2
PGM0015

25

Duck and Run – 7 – 4
PGM0015

26

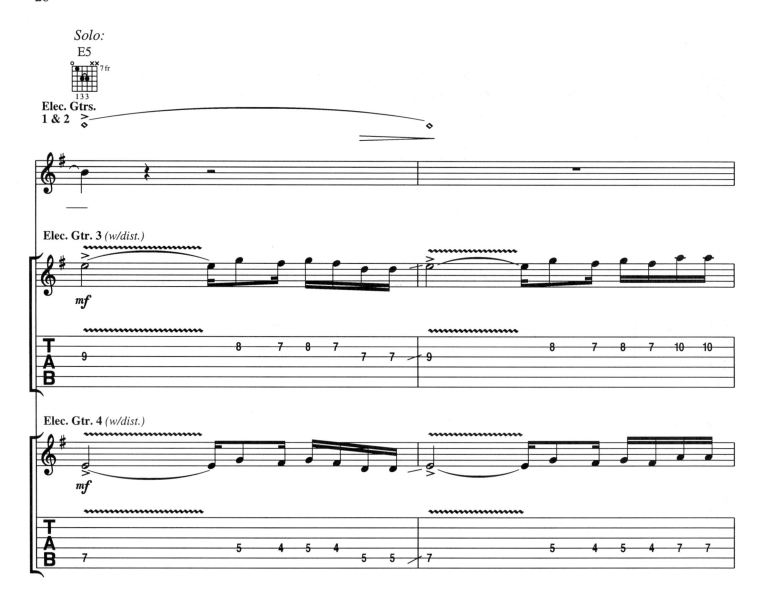

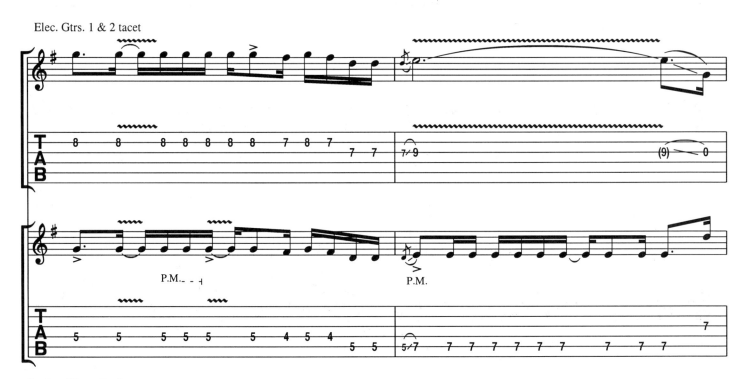

Duck and Run – 7 – 5
PGM0015

NOT ENOUGH

Music by MATT ROBERTS, BRAD ARNOLD,
TODD HARRELL and CHRIS HENDERSON
Lyrics by BRAD ARNOLD

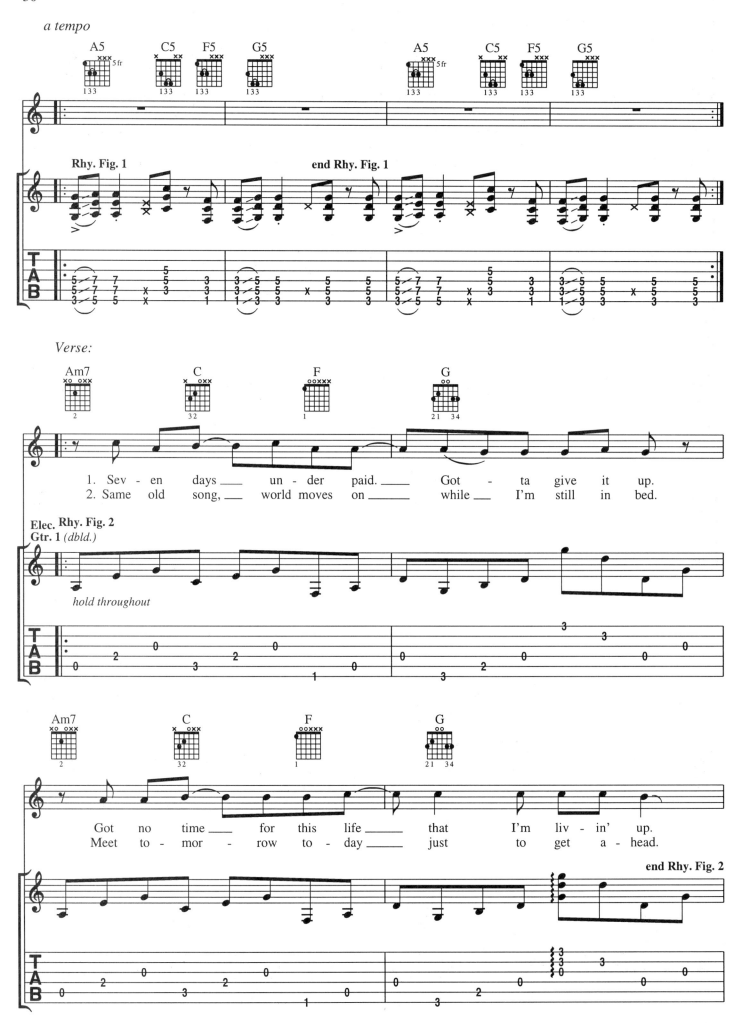

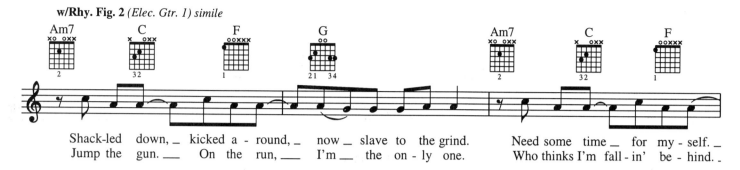

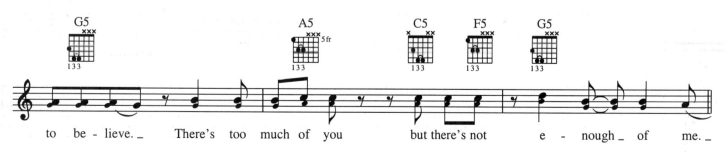

32

34

Chorus:

w/Rhy. Fig. 1 *(Elec. Gtrs. 3 & 4) 4 times, simile*

Not Enough – 7 – 6
PGM0015

BE LIKE THAT

Music by CHRIS HENDERSON
and BRAD ARNOLD
Lyrics by BRAD ARNOLD

38

Be Like That – 8 – 3
PGM0015

he ___ looks up ___ with a lit - tle smile at me ___ and he ___ says,
That's all she needs. Yeah.

Chorus:

Acous. Gtr. 1

Cont. rhy. simile

"If I could be like that, _____ well, I would give an - y - thing ___

Rhy. Fig. 2A

41

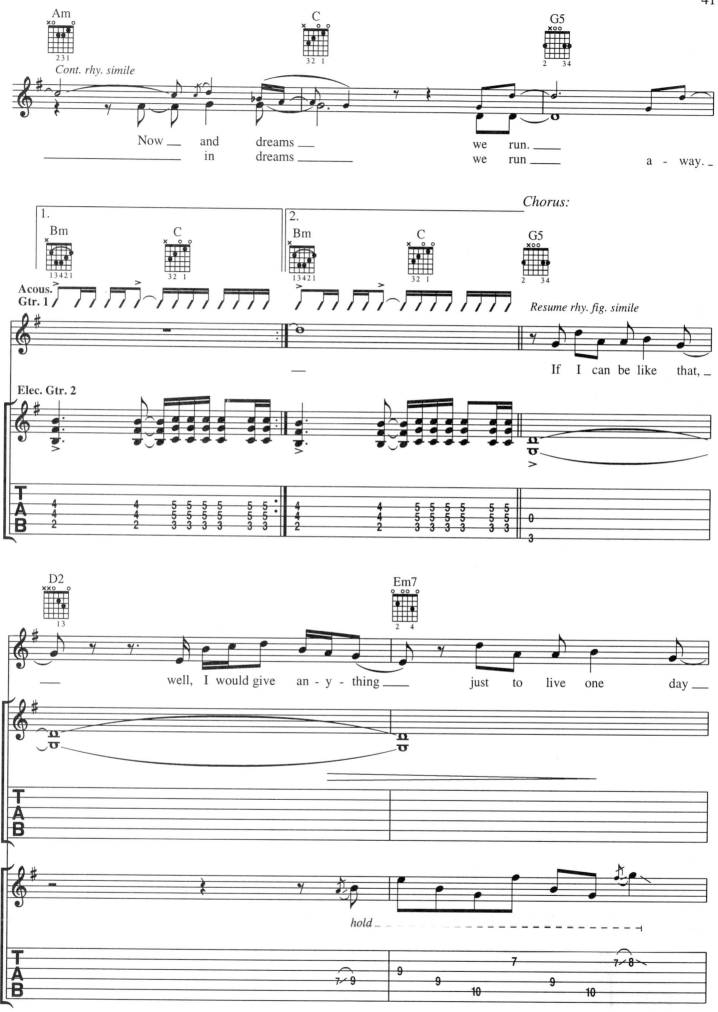

Be Like That – 8 – 6
PGM0015

42

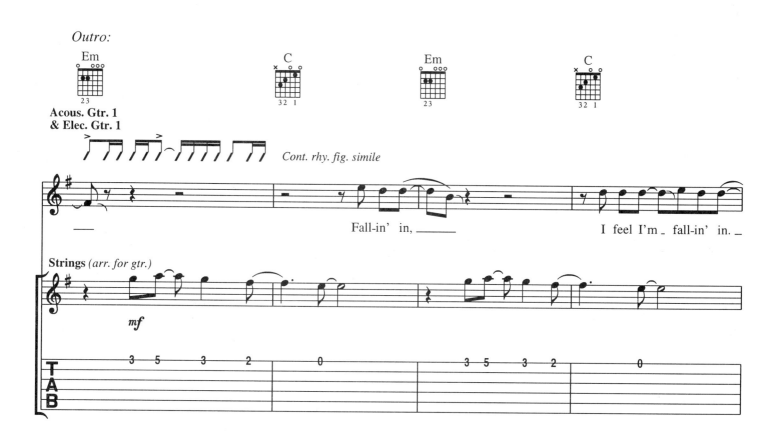

Be Like That – 8 – 8
PGM0015

43

LIFE OF MY OWN

Music by MATT ROBERTS,
BRAD ARNOLD and TODD HARRELL
Lyrics by BRAD ARNOLD

*Implied harmony.

life. ___ (echo repeats)

46

Life of My Own – 7 – 3
PGM0015

48

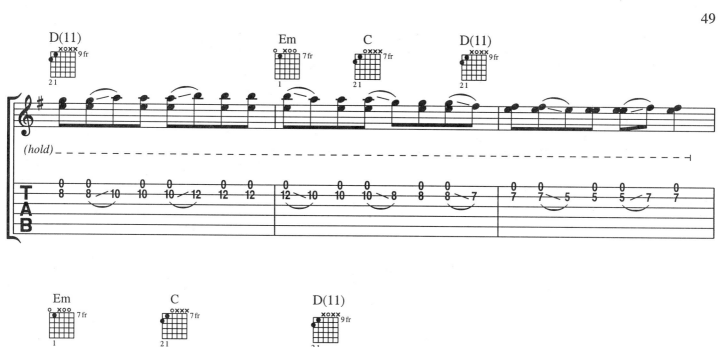

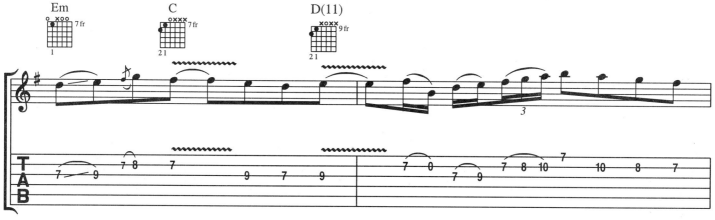

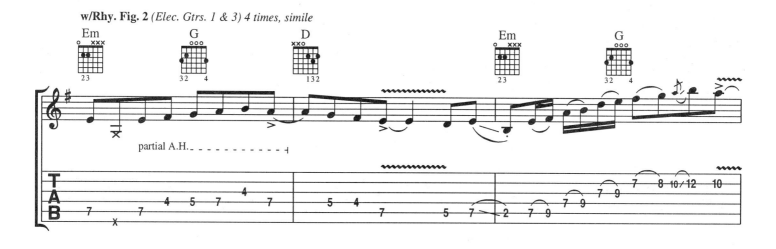

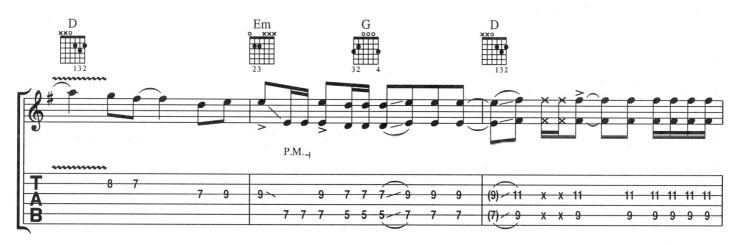

Life of My Own – 7 – 6
PGM0015

50

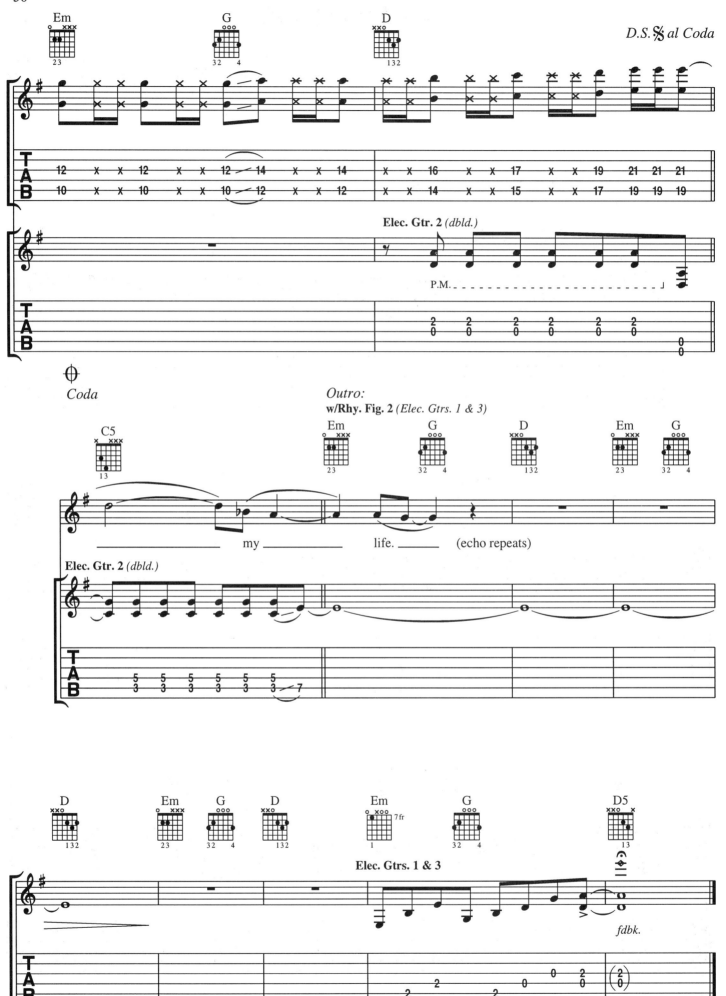

Life of My Own – 7 – 7
PGM0015

BETTER LIFE

Music by MATT ROBERTS, BRAD ARNOLD,
TODD HARRELL and CHRIS HENDERSON
Lyrics by BRAD ARNOLD

Better Life – 8 – 1
PGM0015

52

Elec. Gtr. 2 Elec. Gtr. 1 tacet 1st time only
N.C.

Verses 1 & 2:

w/Rhy. Fig. 1 *(Elec. Gtrs. 1 & 2) simile*
N.C.

1. Well, I'm a-bout to be _____ on the floor a-gain. _ Sure-ly you're gon-na
2. Well, I'm a-bout to see _____ just how far I can fly. _ Sure-ly you're gon-na

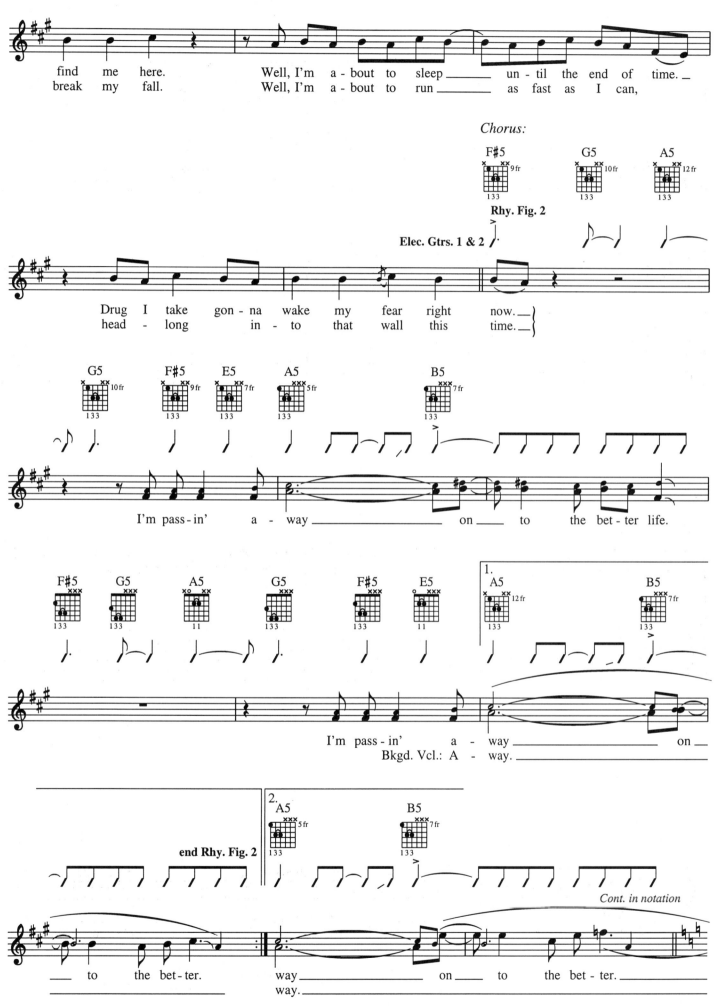

Interlude:

*Composite arrangement.

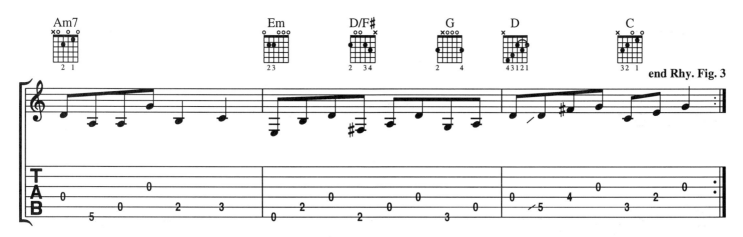

Guitar Solo: Half-time feel

w/Rhy. Fig. 3 *(Elec. Gtrs. 1 & 2) 1 1/2 times, simile*

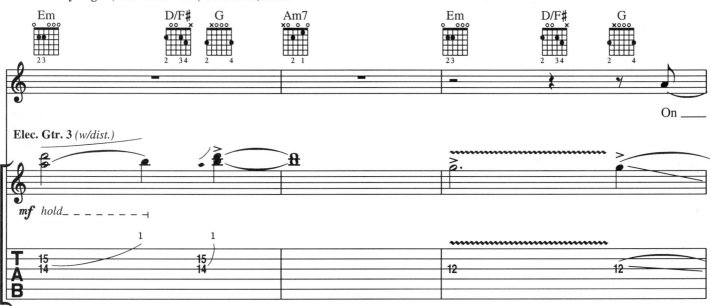

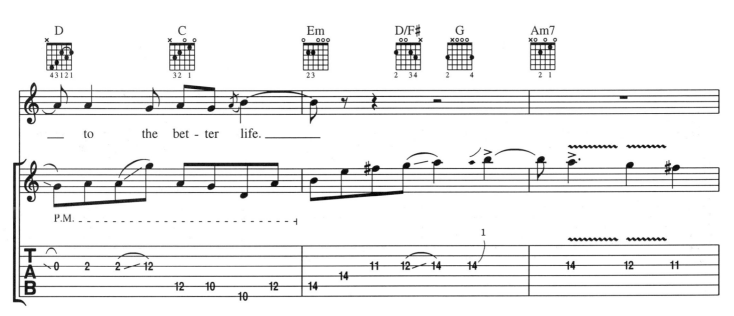

Better Life – 8 – 5
PGM0015

56

On — to the bet-ter.

I'm a-bout to be ____

Elec. Gtrs. 1 & 2

Elec. Gtr. 2 (w/dist.)

Elec. Gtr. 1 (w/dist.)

hold

a tempo
Verse 3:
N.C.

Elec. Gtr. 1

Better Life – 8 – 6
PGM0015

on the floor a-gain._ Sure-ly you're gon-na find me here.

Elec. Gtr. 2

Well, I'm a-bout to sleep _ un-til the end of time. _ Drug I take gon-na wake my fear right

Elec. Gtrs. 1 & 2

Chorus:

w/Rhy. Fig. 2 *(Elec. Gtrs. 1 & 2) simile*

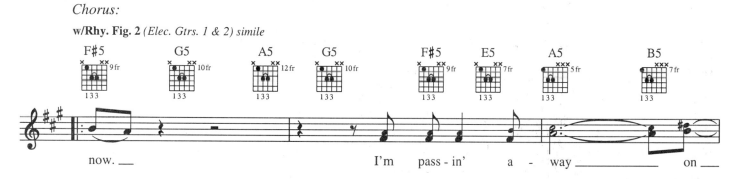

F#5   G5   A5   G5   F#5   E5   A5   B5

now. _   I'm pass-in' a - way ____ on _

58

DOWN POISON

Music by MATT ROBERTS, BRAD ARNOLD,
TODD HARRELL and CHRIS HENDERSON
Lyrics by BRAD ARNOLD

*Composite arrangement.

**Arranged for 6-string gtr.

Elec. Gtrs. 1 & 2 fade out

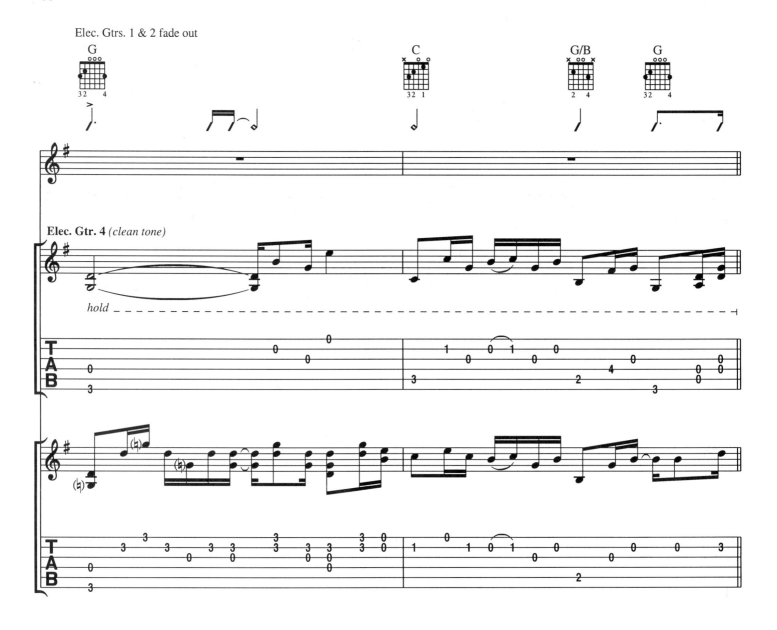

Verse 1:

I've dreamed a-bout_ this _____ for six - teen days_ a -

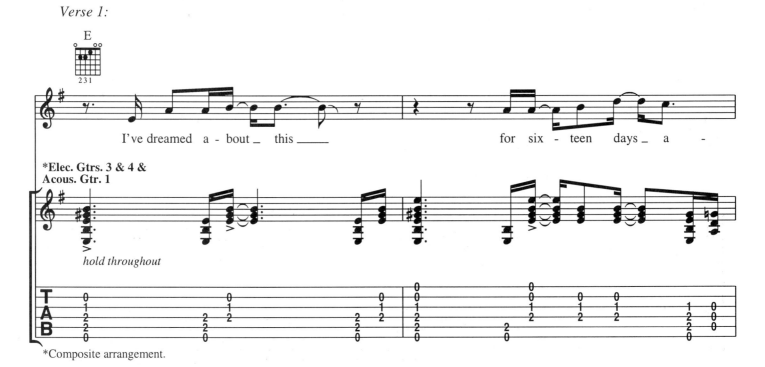

*Composite arrangement.

Down Poison – 8 – 4
PGM0015

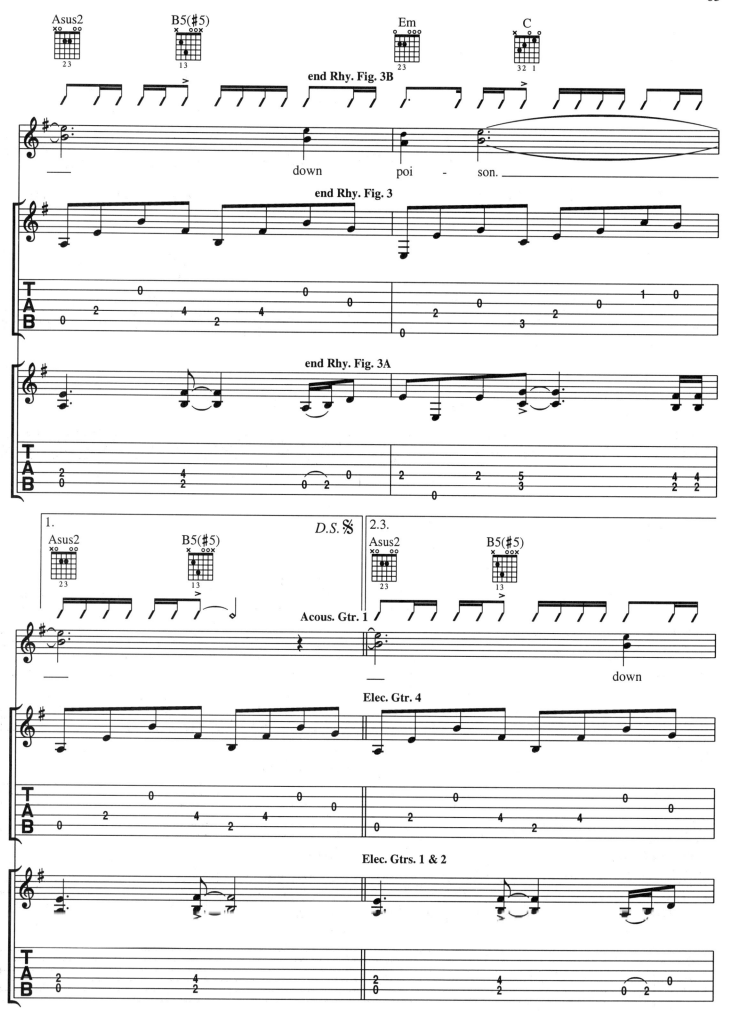

64

Down Poison – 8 – 6
PGM0015

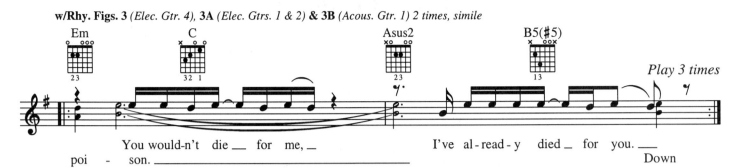

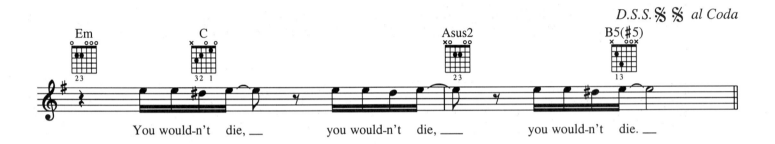

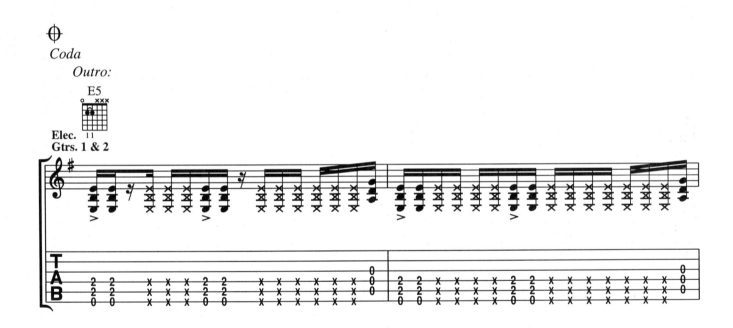

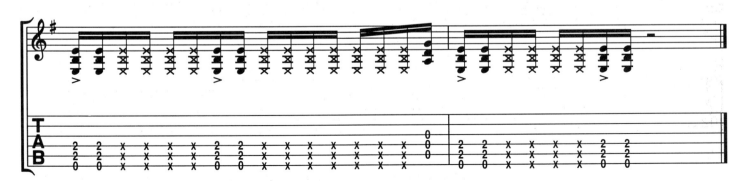

Down Poison – 8 – 8
PGM0015

BY MY SIDE

Music by MATT ROBERTS,
BRAD ARNOLD and TODD HARRELL
Lyrics by BRAD ARNOLD

By My Side - 8 - 1
PGM0015

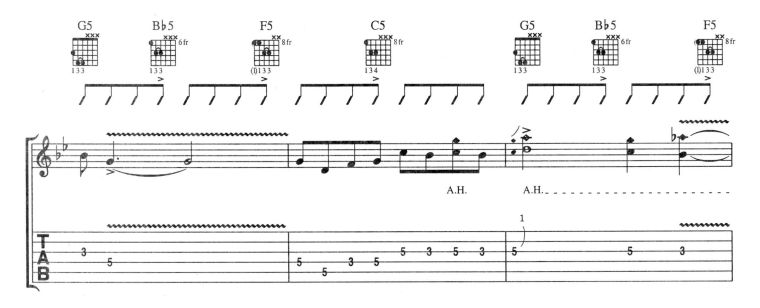

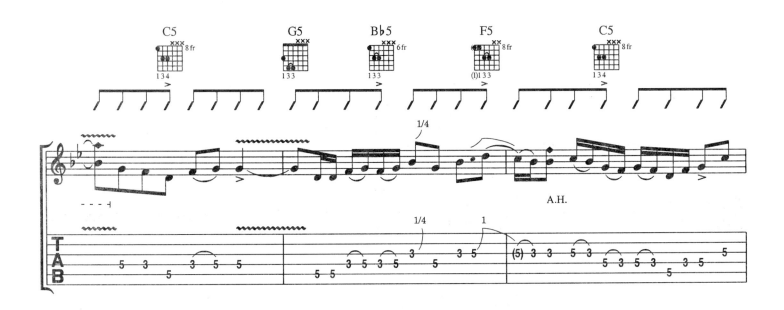

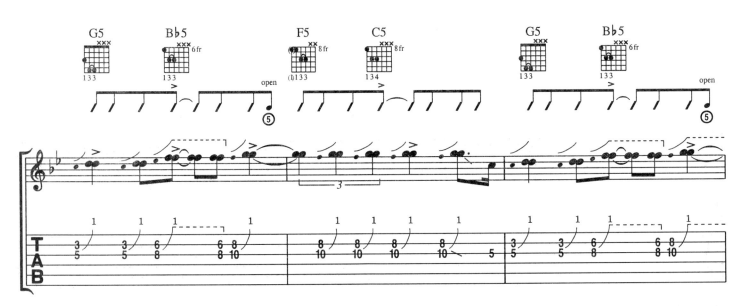

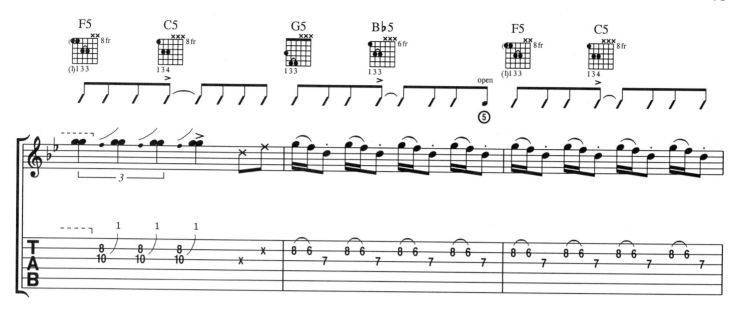

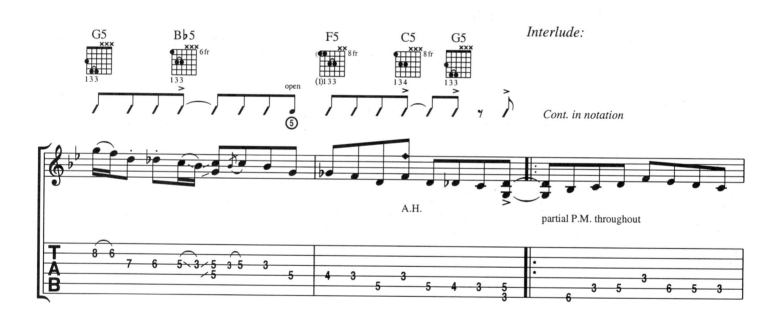

Interlude:

Cont. in notation

A.H.

partial P.M. throughout

By My Side – 8 – 5
PGM0015

72

Chorus:

Well, this could be ___ the last ___ time ___ you ___ will stand ___ by my ___ side. ___ Well, I can feel ___ my soul, ___ it's bleed - ing. Will you fly ___

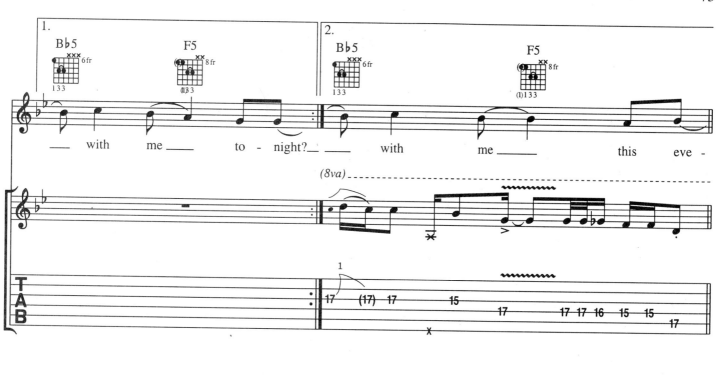

Interlude:
w/Riff A *(Elec. Gtr. 1)*

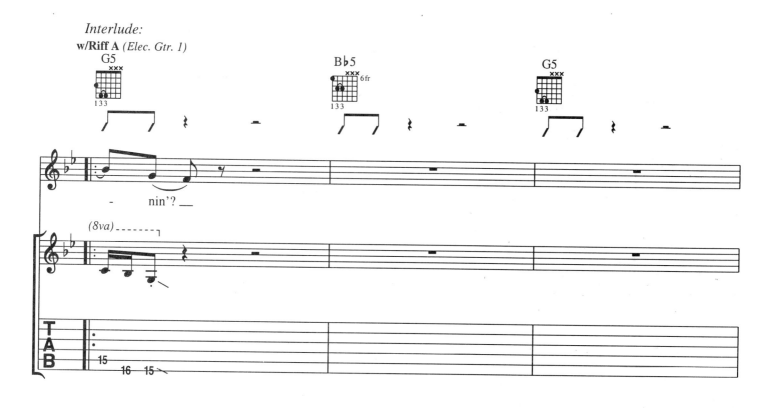

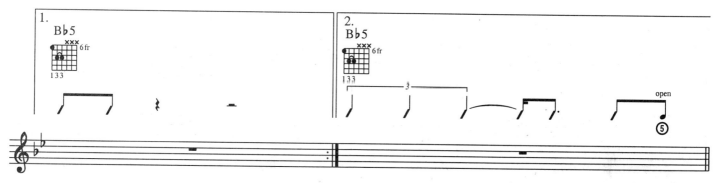

74

Outro:

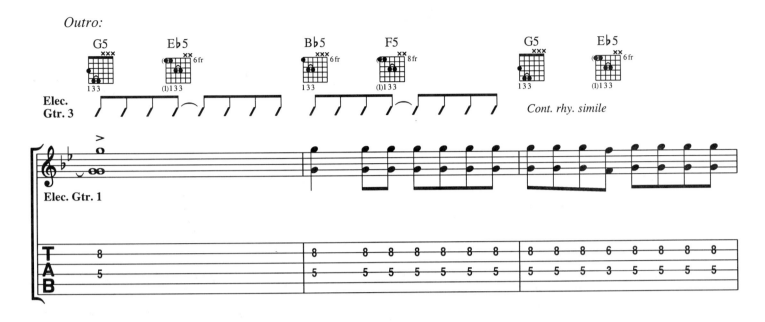

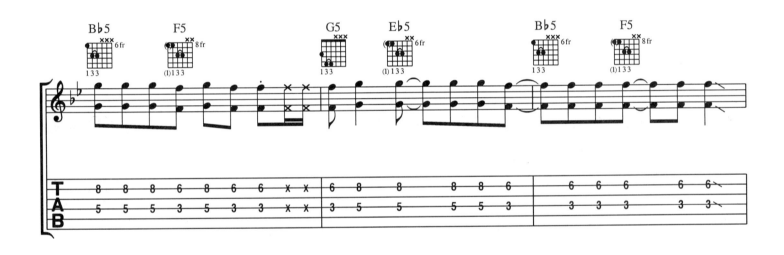

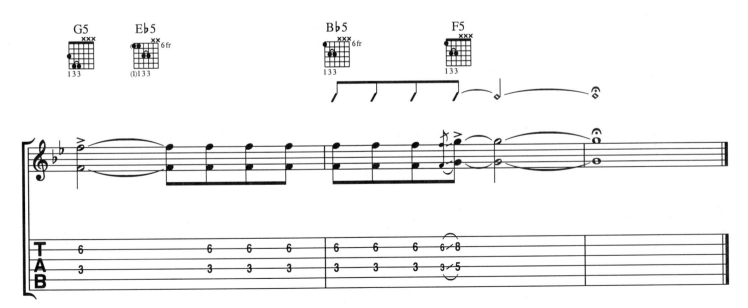

By My Side – 8 – 8
PGM0015

SMACK

Music by MATT ROBERTS,
BRAD ARNOLD and TODD HARRELL
Lyrics by BRAD ARNOLD

Smack – 4 – 1
PGM0015

76

Verses 1 & 2:

1. Rub - ber head - ed mo - tor junk - y, run me down _ and try to stomp me.
2. Trip and fall, _ I'm sure you all can tell me what is on the wall be -

*Elec. Gtrs.
1 & 2   Rhy. Fig. 2

partial P.M. throughout

*Composite arrangement.

Throw my life _ a - way _ and I'll be worth-less just like _____ you. _
hind the li - quor store _ where you get smacked up all the _____ time. _

end Rhy. Fig. 2

78

Smack – 4 – 4
PGM0015

SO I NEED YOU

Music by MATT ROBERTS, BRAD ARNOLD,
TODD HARRELL and CHRIS HENDERSON
Lyrics by BRAD ARNOLD

Moderately fast ♩ = 140

Intro:

Em7   D(4,9)   C   C(9)   B5

Elec. Gtr. 1 *(clean tone)*

mf hold

Elec. Gtr. 2 *(w/dist.)*

mf partial P.M.

E5   D5   E5   D5

Elec. Gtr. 4 *(w/dist.)*   **Elec. Gtr. 4**

Elec. Gtr. 1

*dbld. by Elec. Gtr. 3 w/dist.   **Rhy. Fig. 1**

P.M. single notes

*Composite arrangement.

So I Need You – 7 – 1
PGM0015

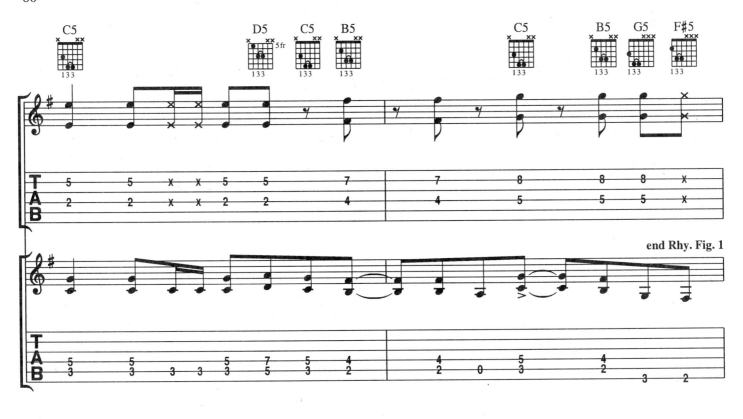

end Rhy. Fig. 1

w/Rhy. Fig. 1 *(Elec. Gtrs. 2 & 3) simile*

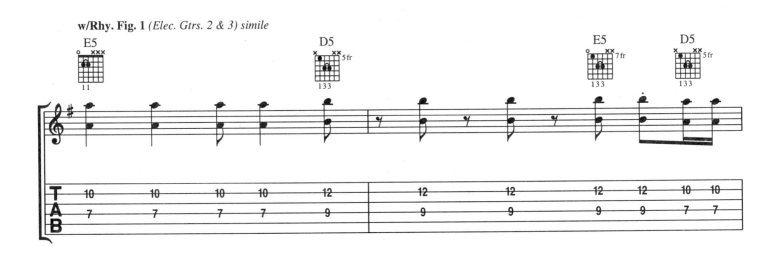

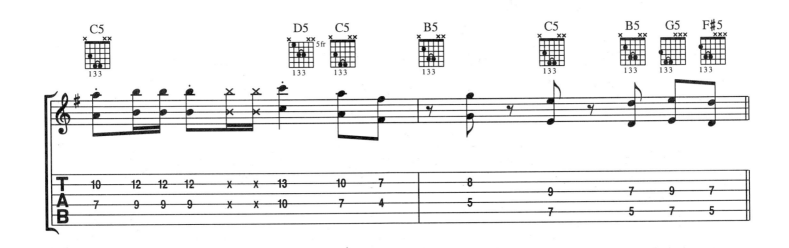

*Composite arrangement.

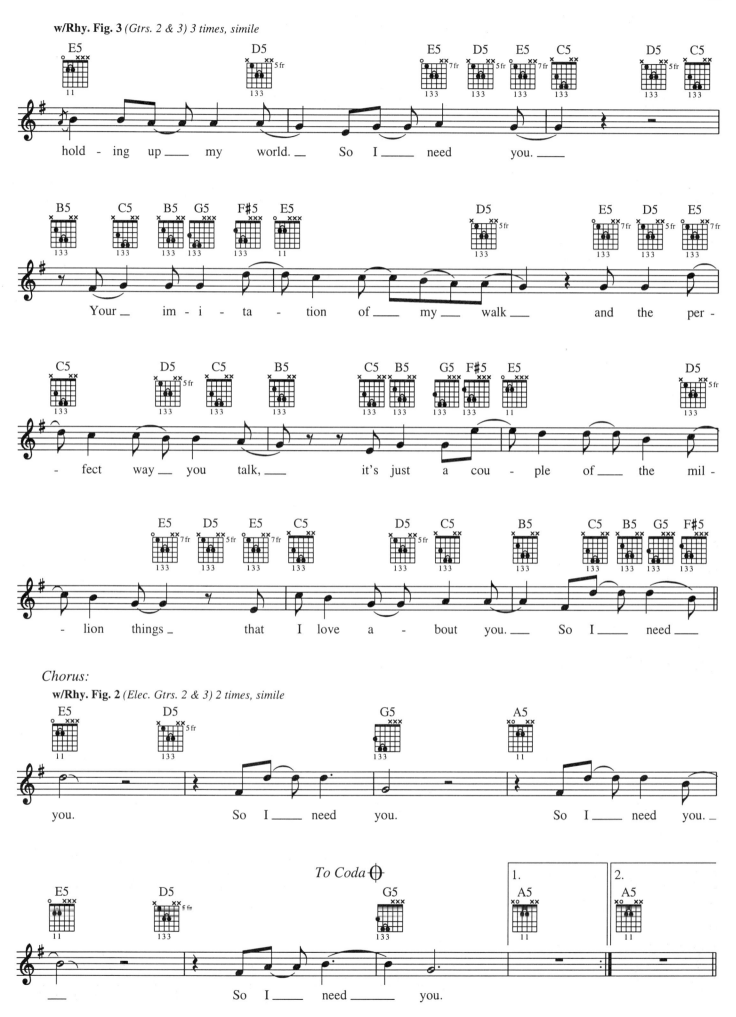

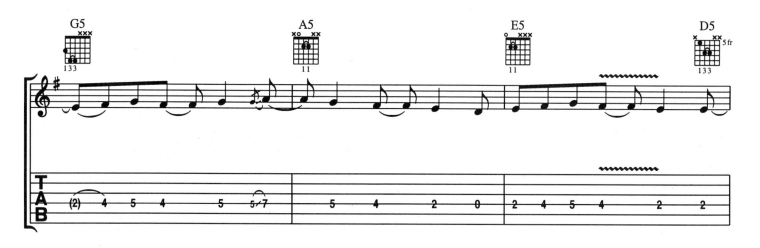

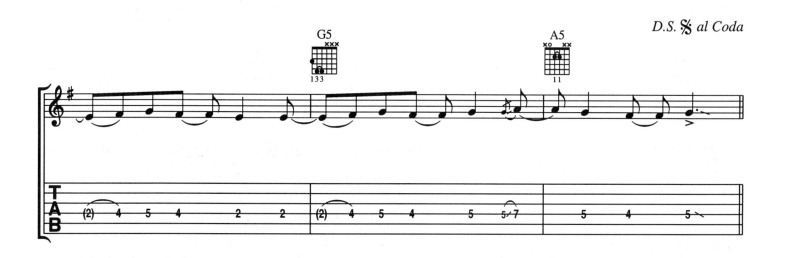

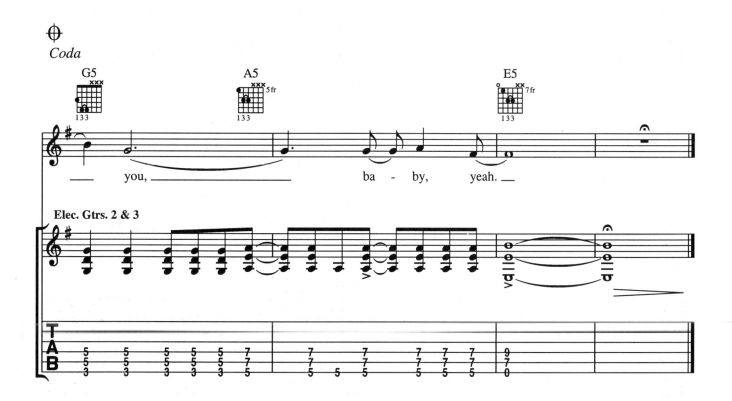

GUITAR TAB GLOSSARY **

TABLATURE EXPLANATION

READING TABLATURE: Tablature illustrates the six strings of the guitar. Notes and chords are indicated by the placement of fret numbers on a given string(s).

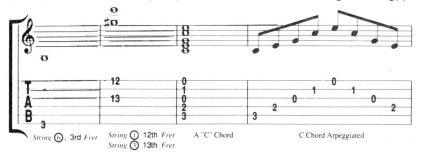

String ⑥, 3rd Fret   String ① 12th Fret   A "C" Chord   C Chord Arpeggiated
String ③ 13th Fret

BENDING NOTES

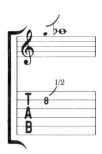

HALF STEP: Play the note and bend string one half step.*

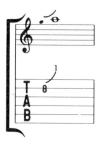

WHOLE STEP: Play the note and bend string one whole step.

WHOLE STEP AND A HALF: Play the note and bend string a whole step and a half.

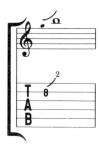

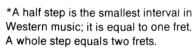

TWO STEPS: Play the note and bend string two whole steps.

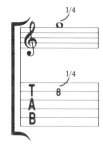

SLIGHT BEND (Microtone): Play the note and bend string slightly to the equivalent of half a fret.

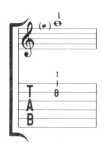

PREBEND (Ghost Bend): Bend to the specified note, before the string is picked.

PREBEND AND RELEASE: Bend the string, play it, then release to the original note.

REVERSE BEND: Play the already-bent string, then immediately drop it down to the fretted note.

BEND AND RELEASE: Play the note and gradually bend to the next pitch, then release to the original note. Only the first note is attacked.

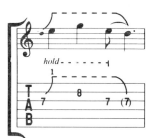

BENDS INVOLVING MORE THAN ONE STRING: Play the note and bend string while playing an additional note (or notes) on another string(s). Upon release, relieve pressure from additional note(s), causing original note to sound alone.

BENDS INVOLVING STATIONARY NOTES: Play notes and bend lower pitch, then hold until release begins (indicated at the point where line becomes solid).

UNISON BEND: Play both notes and immediately bend the lower note to the same pitch as the higher note.

DOUBLE NOTE BEND: Play both notes and immediately bend both strings simultaneously.

*A half step is the smallest interval in Western music; it is equal to one fret. A whole step equals two frets.

© 1990 Beam Me Up Music
c/o CPP/Belwin, Inc. Miami, Florida 33014
International Copyright Secured   Made in U.S.A.   All Rights Reserved   **By Kenn Chipkin and Aaron Stang

RHYTHM SLASHES

STRUM INDICATIONS: Strum with indicated rhythm. The chord voicings are found on the first page of the transcription underneath the song title.

INDICATING SINGLE NOTES USING RHYTHM SLASHES: Very often single notes are incorporated into a rhythm part. The note name is indicated above the rhythm slash with a fret number and a string indication.

ARTICULATIONS

HAMMER ON: Play lower note, then "hammer on" to higher note with another finger. Only the first note is attacked.

LEFT HAND HAMMER: Hammer on the first note played on each string with the left hand.

PULL OFF: Play higher note, then "pull off" to lower note with another finger. Only the first note is attacked.

FRETBOARD TAPPING: "Tap" onto the note indicated by + with a finger of the pick hand, then pull off to the following note held by the fret hand.

TAP SLIDE: Same as fretboard tapping, but the tapped note is slid randomly up the fretboard, then pulled off to the following note.

BEND AND TAP TECHNIQUE: Play note and bend to specified interval. While holding bend, tap onto note indicated.

LEGATO SLIDE: Play note and slide to the following note. (Only first note is attacked).

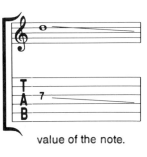

LONG GLISSANDO: Play note and slide in specified direction for the full value of the note.

SHORT GLISSANDO: Play note for its full value and slide in specified direction at the last possible moment.

PICK SLIDE: Slide the edge of the pick in specified direction across the length of the string(s).

MUTED STRINGS: A percussive sound is made by laying the fret hand across all six strings while pick hand strikes specified area (low, mid, high strings).

PALM MUTE: The note or notes are muted by the palm of the pick hand by lightly touching the string(s) near the bridge.

TREMOLO PICKING: The note or notes are picked as fast as possible.

TRILL: Hammer on and pull off consecutively and as fast as possible between the original note and the grace note.

ACCENT: Notes or chords are to be played with added emphasis.

STACCATO (Detached Notes): Notes or chords are to be played roughly half their actual value and with separation.

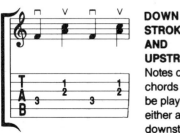

DOWN STROKES AND UPSTROKES: Notes or chords are to be played with either a downstroke (⊓ ·) or upstroke (∨) of the pick.

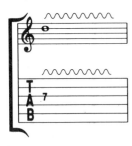

VIBRATO: The pitch of a note is varied by a rapid shaking of the fret hand finger, wrist, and forearm.

HARMONICS

NATURAL HARMONIC: A finger of the fret hand lightly touches the note or notes indicated in the tab and is played by the pick hand.

ARTIFICIAL HARMONIC: The first tab number is fretted, then the pick hand produces the harmonic by using a finger to lightly touch the same string at the second tab number (in parenthesis) and is then picked by another finger.

ARTIFICIAL "PINCH" HARMONIC: A note is fretted as indicated by the tab, then the pick hand produces the harmonic by squeezing the pick firmly while using the tip of the index finger in the pick attack. If parenthesis are found around the fretted note, it does not sound. No parenthesis means both the fretted note and A.H. are heard simultaneously.

TREMOLO BAR

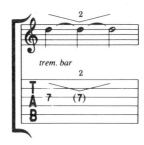

SPECIFIED INTERVAL: The pitch of a note or chord is lowered to a specified interval and then may or may not return to the original pitch. The activity of the tremolo bar is graphically represented by peaks and valleys.

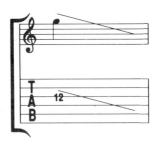

UN-SPECIFIED INTERVAL: The pitch of a note or a chord is lowered to an unspecified interval.